CW00552951

THE 'AZARDS O' CHIMUCK SZWIPPIN

and
other poems

by

Keith Morgan

Illustrated by Doug Eaton

Keith Morgan

Published by Douglas McLean
at
The Forest Bookshop
8 St. John Street, Coleford,
Gloucestershire, GL16 8AR

This edition published in Great Britain by

DOUGLAS McLEAN
at
The Forest Bookshop
8 St. John Street, Coleford,
Gloucestershire, GL16 8AR
1999

ISBN 0 946252 45 9

Printed in Great Britain by
Copyplus of Monmouth   Tel: 01600 772600

Whether writing or reciting his poetry in Forest dialect or Queen's English, Keith Morgan never fails to delight his audience with the originality and vitality of his verse, which skilfully captures the humour and passion of the Forester for posterity.

Keith Morgan was born in 1942 and has lived all his life in Coleford in the Forest of Dean. He attended St. John's Primary and Bell's Grammar schools. He now runs a traditional barbershop in the centre of Coleford which, he readily admits, is a rich source of many of his yarns.

This collection originally appeared in two separate books *The 'Azards 'o Chimuck Szwippin'* and *Albert's Dree Wiker*.

Contents

Foreword

I little dreamed when *The 'Azards o' Chimuck Szwippin* was first published in 1978 that it would create the interest that it did. Some of the poems have been set to music. Some reappeared in National publications and others such a *Varest Ship* became well known, more for the title than the content.

The popularity of the poems and the humour contained in many of them, has meant that I am often requested to give 'after-dinner speeches', which I enjoy most of all. I also came to realise just how many Women's Institute groups there are around Gloucestershire and its surrounding counties. It was at a W.I. gathering in Herefordshire that I was introduced as '....that well-known chimney sweep from the Forest of Dean'!

Today, the Forest people retain their humour but the dialect is fast disappearing. I am more likely to be asked by a young customer in my Coleford barber's shop to 'fin me 'air aht mate' than to 'gissa good trim awld butty'. This is sad but inevitable. However, I am happy to have done my bit to record the Forest dialect for posterity.

My interest in writing came from my years at Coleford's long since closed Bell's Grammar School, and I am indebted to my English master, the late Colin Evans for the tremendous encouragement he gave me in those days.

In later years, the late Harry Beddington (in my consideration, the finest writer of the Forest dialect), became a good friend and mentor and the poet and writer, the late Leonard Clark, was also inspirational and personally gave me much encouragement.

I am naturally delighted that my two collections are now re-published in this volume. My thanks for this go to Doug McLean of the Forest Bookshop and to my illustrator Doug Eaton. I trust now that a new generation of readers may enjoy them and that my old readers will take pleasure from them again.

The history of the Forest of Dean is that of a people of great independence and here are a few lines from me that reflect this and also offer a suggestion for our own emblem:

Scotland has the thistle
England wears the rose
Holland has the tulip
Wales the 'daffy' chose
The French have their fleur-de-lys
Ireland the shamrock green
But here - deep in the Forest
The 'Snomper'* is supreme

*Foxglove

Keith Morgan, Coleford, 1999

UP FER THE CUP

IF thee bist fond o' aggro
  Then thee con watch a yup,
When Drybruk da ploy Yarkley
  In thic Combination Cup.

Chunt a game fer faint 'earts
  An them as 'ate it 'ot,
Cos thee will 'ave thee vill
  O' blood an' tith an' snot.

When blokes run on ta meadow
  'Tis the 'orriblest sight I've seen,
Thirty gummy players
  Stinkin' o' wintergreen.

Thic ref 'ims on a loser
  Whatever 'im da do,
'An the only reason 'e be there
  Is cos no one else 'ould goo.

Thic whistle blows out sharply
  Ta start the wretched game,
An' seconds a'ter startin'
  Seven o' the backs be lame.

They'd bin daft enough ta run the ball
  Which byunt in Forest rules,
And delicately wus stamped upon
  By a pack o' maraudin' mules.

Then the packs thoy settled down
  Ta prove their strength an' might,
An 'appily ployed the 'ole fust 'alf
  Wi'out a ball in sight.

The vust aid mon were busy
  Wi' 'is needle an' 'is thread,
Stitchin' on bits an' sartin' out
  The livin' from the dead.

The crowd wus warmin' to it now
  Bellowin' wi' all their might,
Some wus cheering': some wus not
  An' dree went off ta fight.

Both sides by now wus caked in mud
  An' some o' the spectators too,
An' soon it wus quite 'ard ta tell
  Just who wus thumpin' who.

Thic ref 'im blew 'is whistle
　Ta end the zorry affair,
But the ployers never 'eard 'n
　An' ployded on wi'out a care.

'Im stuck 'is yud into the scrum
　Ta tell 'em it were over,
They dragged 'n in an' chucked 'n out
　Wi'out 'is pants fer cover.

Thoy stopped the game an' all shook 'ands
　The score wus nought a-piece,
An' agreed that till the reploy
　The violence 'ould cease.

Thoy washed an' changed an' got their tith
　From a box nailed ta the wall,
Then trooped off ta the local
　Ta swile it in 'em all.

Thoy swiled it in 'em solid
　From five till 'alf past ten,
Some wus sick an' some wus not
　But few could care by then.

Thoy sang an' cussed an' blinded
　An' 'ad their ale on "tick"
An' all agreed amongst their selves
　They'd ploy agen next wik.

PIE YUTTIN'

IF thee's ever 'ear a story
                'bout a mon wi appetite,
Do'sn't disbelieve un
                'cause thee's be sure 'im's right.
It 'appened late one evening
                in the bar o' thic Nags Yud,
Old Charlie 'im felt 'ungry
                tho' 'twern't long since 'im were fed.
"Don't yer missus feed ya?"
                one rosy faced gent said,
"Oh aye; but that were 'our ago
                since last I 'ad me bread".
"Zurry", said another,
                "If thee's yut as much as that,
Thee's wunt get through thic door at night;
                yer'll be too blinkin' fat."
"Yuttin' is me 'obby",
                old Charlie did reply,

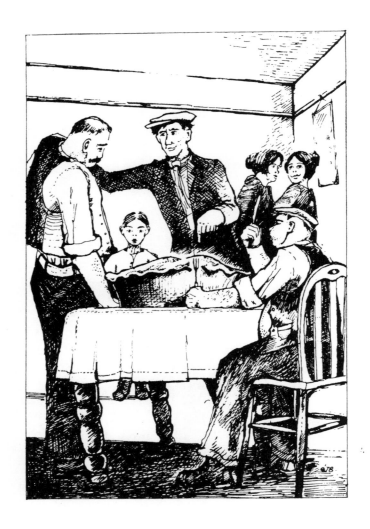

"An' if there's summut wuth a yuttin'
                    'tis a steak and kydney pie".
'Is mates got their yuds together
                    and readily agreed,
That they'd make old Chal a pastry,
                    mar than 'im ould need.
One's missus made the pastry,
                    another found the dish,
Someone brought two pound o' steak,
                    another three o' fish.
They put it in the pastry dish
                    an' placed upon the top,
Tomatoes, greens an' cucumber
                    and a greasy gert lamb chop.
They laced the lot wi mongee*,
                    an' put the top on tight,
An' put 'im in the oven
                    an' cooked un over night.
When they took 'n out next marnin'
                    'im were done right to a turn,
The pastry wus quite crispy
                    where the sides began ta burn.
Thoy took thic pie ta Charlie
                    and set 'n on the table
An' said ta 'im in mockin' tone,
                    "Yut thic if thee bist able!"
'Im looked at it; an sniffed at it
                    an' loosened off 'is belt,
An' commented upon thic pie;
                    the best as 'e ad smelt.
'E removed the top an' looked around
                    ta see what 'im ad got,

* blancmange

7

Then took a breath an' dived right in;
     an' yut the bloody lot.
'Is mates looked on in disbelief
     as Charlie wiped the plate,
For im' 'ad yut in 'alf an hour
     enough fer twenty-eight.
Chal sat back contented like
     an' smacked 'is lips wi pride,
Then suddenly 'is face turned green
     an' so did 'is inside,
Through the door 'im went flat out
     and raced out through the trees,
'Is 'and was clasped across 'is mouth,
     an' 'is trousers round 'is knees.
'Im were in thic wood all a'ternoon
     an' well into the night,
An' all 'is mates were doubled up
     at Charlie's sorry plight.
When finally 'im got off wum,
     'is tea were on the table,
'E looked at it an' sniffed at it;
     but yut it 'im weren't able.
So off to bed old Charlie went,
     an' three 'ole days did stay,
An' never again did Charlie boast
     o' what 'im could put away.

LINES WRITTEN IN
COLEFORD CEMETERY, 1971

OH, tangled mess of weed and thorn
   What place is this to rest,
When three score years and ten are served
   Is it with you we're blessed?

Does every year of toil and strain
   Of hardships, trials and tears,
End in this; a matted bed
   To spend the silent years?

No doubt in bygone day you bore
   A far more splendid cloak,
   Before the flowers began to die
And weed began to choke.

Oh, craggy stones how long you've stood
    The tempest and the storm,
How age hath taken toll of you
    How deep your face be worn.

We can but guess whose rest you guard
    Whose name you bear with pride,
The question asked of every stone
    Just who are they that died?

A farmer or a carpenter
    A banker or a clerk,
A soldier or a little child
    All sleeping 'neath the dark.

Names long since vanished from the grave
    Their station counts no more,
Weak and mighty side by side
    With wealthy and with poor.

Around their graves the weed entwines
    The grass is green no more,
The thorn bush wraps around the head
    Just like the crown He wore.

Oh, tangled mess of weed and thorn
    A peace they've found in you,
Where we who die may come to rest
    And I will lie here to.

HERITAGE

Salute blithe bearers of heritage, so
Festooned in the ribbons of lore,
Gaily pursuing traditions of old
Conceived in the labyrinth of yore.

MIRACLE IN A CLOUDBURST

Small Sally in the meadow
Culling the fresh through blooms of Spring,
The sun blesses.
Small Sally in the meadow;
Vacant to all but the pleasures of Spring;
Heaven sent.
Small Sally in the meadow
Feeling the sudden damp of cloudburst sky,
Running through sodden grass — wet tears
Falling on wet earth.
The church porch.
Shelter from teeming endless rain that
beats down on that once tranquil
pastoral scene.
Small Sally in the porch
Crying the endless tears of hurt.
The rain beats.

Small Sally lifts her head,
Perceives a candle light
Beckoning — calling — hypnotically
Drawing the child into
Its warm comfort glow.
Small Sally in the aisle
Gazing wonderously — bathed in the mellow
Tallow glow.
The rain torrents against the stained glass saints.
Small Sally turns,
Sees the brass-oak tablet bathed now
In candle light, and reads —
"Suffer little children to come unto me and forbid
Them not for their's is the Kingdom of Heaven."
A shaft of light.
Beaming through stained glass
Awash with rain bathing
The child in its tender comfort wrap.
Small Sally comforted
Dry as the child that gathered the blooms
Before the storm.
Small Sally in the meadow,
The rains ceased. The sun beaming down as
The summer blooms are gathered once more
Into the hands of a child.

A PLEA

Rᴀɪsᴇ me up ethereal wings
　　From slumber let me wake,
Liberate my soul from things
　　So alien to my sake.

Refract my "wake" to planes which now
　　Are closed to shuttered mind,
Take me from this earthly slough
　　Of pathways walked by blind.

Let me be as "all around"
　　Observing mortal self,
Free as freedom knows no bounds
　　Divorced of earthly wealth.

PIG ON THE WALL

SIDDY and Jummy were sat on a wall
  A pig was a mootin' close by,
When "Onward" came oompahing down the
                         main street
An' the folks rushed ta watch 'em march by.
"Beautiful music" said one bloke ta t'other,
"The best in the Forest", Sid said,
An' thic pig stopped mootin an' cocked up 'is ear
Then 'e lifted 'is gert ugly 'ead.
T'were as if the fine music 'ad got through ta 'im
An 'ad registered deep in 'is brain,
"I think thic pig's fond o' some Sousa", said Jim,
As thic pig squealed out as if in pain.
'Im squealed in time ta the beat o' the band,
An' 'e danced around there on the ground,
'Twere the funniest thing as they ever 'ad sin
For a musical pig they 'ad found.

16

As Onward got nearer the pig jumped up 'igh
Ta try ta see over the wall,
But 'twere to no avail fer thic wall was quite 'igh
An' thic pig 'im were not very tall.
As the second carnet player played a lovely B flat
Thic pig 'im got inter a state,
Im rolled on the ground wi 'is vit in the air
An' looked at thic wall vull o' 'ate.
The trombonist blew out a brilliant quaver
The sart that the village weren't used ta,
But thic pig was beside 'isself now as 'e clawed
At thic wall between 'im an' old Sousa.
Siddy looked at Jummy an' Jummy at Sid
An' both in turn scratched at 'is 'at,
"Perhaps", said Jummy, "Im would quieten down
If up on these wall 'im were sat".
"Perhaps thee be right", old Siddy replied
As 'e gave thic old pig a call,
An' together they lifted 'im up in the air
An' sat 'im on top of thic wall.
Now when 'e were sat on the top o' thic wall
'E were able ta see 'em at last,
'E sat there content wi 'is yud in the air
An' 'e watched thic old brass band go past.

WORDS TO A CURIOUS LAD
ON REMEMBRANCE SUNDAY

Y ES lad they were young boys
  Those names upon that stone,
Where silent people gather now
  In memory of their own.
Where naught but sorrow haunts the air
  'cept p'rhaps a sense of pride,
Yes pride and sorrow still remain
  But not the boys who died.

Yes lad they are forgotten
  By all 'cept just a few,
Like those that stand before us
  The fathers they once new.
Parents who had raised from birth
  Those sons so dear to them,
Fathers who now stand and share
  This silent requiem.

No lad they were not heroes
　　By any choice of their's,
Nor did they seek the glory
　　That the hero proudly wears.
They simply did their duty
　　To keep these Islands free,
They died for that one precious aim
　　They died for you and me.

COME MY LOVE

Come my love and walk with me
   Through meadows flowered and green,
Where cattle graze and wild bird swim
   On waters still — serene.

Come my love and take my hand
   And walk the river's edge,
'long mossy banks — 'neath weeping boughs
   Through reed and rush and sedge.

Come my love and climb with me
   To view the distant hills,
Beyond the leafy forests where
   White cloud the blue sky fills.

Come my love and sit with me
   Beneath the oak tree's shade,
Where beach and elm and chestnut grace
   Each cool romantic glade.

Come my love and tell me of
   The beauties you have seen,
All in a day spent wandering
   In this our lovely Dean.

THE BATTLE OF COLEFORD

IN thic Kings Yud thoy were sat
                  a suppin' at their ale,
When in rushed a lad from Monmouth
                  an' blurted out this tale,
"Lord 'Erbert's down in Monmouth
                  wi' a thousand mon I'd say,
An' judgin' by their guns an' things
                  thoy byunt there fer market day".
"Lord 'Erbert!" said a tippler,
                  " 'Im's in King Charles's poy",
"Oy, an' thee's con watch thee step
                  'im's a yuddin' up thee's woy".
"An 'im can 'ave some knuckle
                  if I da clap me 'ands on 'im",
Said Rube, a swarthy Forester
                  thick in yud an' mind an' limb.

"Thic King 'ave gave our rights awoy,
                    our woods an' mines; the lot,
An' if thee's wunt my opinion
                    thic blighter should be shot".
"Well spoken", said a voice
                    from a corner of the inn,
"Colonel Berrowe is my name,
                    let me rope you fellows in.
I've got fifty Parliamentary troops
                    positioned down the road,
And if you chaps would lend a hand
                    it would help to share the load".
By now the ale wus talkin'
                    an' thoy all wus feelin' brave,
Thoy volunteered ta 'ave a go
                    an' each a gun was gave.
Some staggered out into the street,
                    the rest thoy stopped inside,
Some felt brave; an' some weren't sure;
                    an' two ran off ta 'ide,
As Charles's troops marched inta town
                    thoy took their aim an' fired,
Thoy fought each other 'and ta 'and
                    till both the sides grew tired.
A Cavalier stopped ta light a fag,
                    an' sat on a bale of straw,
'E drapped 'is match into the hay,
                    an' burnt the old Town 'All.
"Zurry!" said Rube, in disbelief,
                    "Thoy be takin' it seriously,
I've 'ad enough; an further more
                    thic pub'll be open at dree".
Thoy'd fought each other tooth an' noil
                    fer near on two 'ole 'ours,

Djud were dree Kings soldiers
                an' a lady sellin' flowers.
Thoy lay down all their weapons
                an' crept back ta thic Kings Yud,
'An agreed among themselves
                as thoy were lucky thoy weren't djud.
"We've 'ad a bloody 'idin' ",
                said Rube ta one an' all,
"An' if I be called ta arms agyun;
                then I shant 'ear thic call.

THE 'AZARDS O'
CHIMUCK SZWIPPIN

'AST ever swep a chimuck
    Ta earn theeself a bob?
Old 'Arry 'ave an' 'im da know
    The 'azards o' thic job.
The neighbour'd 'ad some soot down
    The biggest pile 'er'd seen,
So 'er decides ta fetch a mon
    Ta szwip thic blighter clean.
'Er goes across ta 'Arry's
    Ta ex 'im if 'e knew,
Of any mon wi' 'our ta spare
    Ta come an' szwip 'er flue.
Old 'Arry thought a minute
    'Bout the merits of the job,
An' come ta the decision
    That 'e could use a bob.
"I'll szwip thee chimuck far tha"
    Old 'Arry volunteered,
"Thou give I couple 'a 'ours
    An' I'll 'ave thic blighter cleared".

'E went off down the village
   An' into local pub,
Ta see if 'im could borra
   The tackle fer the job.
"What bist thee a gwine ta do?"
   One aged drinker said,
"T'aint like thee ta look fer work
   Bist gwine ta szwip thee bed?"
"Thee asn't worked fer ages"
   Another did reply,
"If thou's lend I rods and brush
   I'll start thee's very day".
"Thee'l find a set at our place"
   Said Alfie, 'Arry's mate,
"An' mind tha's treat 'em wi' respect
   An' don't ferget the date".
Off 'Arry goes ta Alfie's
   Ta fetch the brush an' sack,
An' gathered up a pile of rods
   An' slung 'em on 'is back.
To 'is neighbours 'e took off
   An' knocked upon the door,
'E took the brushes from 'is back
   An' slung 'em on the floor.
'E picked a rod an' brush up
   An' one ta t'other did screw,
Then took 'em to the fireplace
   An' stuffed 'em up the flue.
'E screwed on some more brushes
   An' turned 'em round about,
But 'alf way up thic chimuck
   A gert red brick fell out.

'Im shouted ta the neighbour
    Ta take a look out back,
An' tell 'im when the brush wus through
    Above the chimney stack.
'Er stood outside an 'our
    But nothing did appear,
Tho' 'Arry'd used up thirty rods
    The top were no'where near.
'Im got up from thic fireplace
    An' shook 'is 'ead in doubt,
"If I've used up all them rods
    Thic blighter should be out".
'Im went down ta the village
    Ta borrow some more poles,
"What bist szwippin' ", one bloke asked,
    "Some blinkin' rabbit's 'oles?"
'Im went back up thic hillside
    An' entered through the door,
An' got down by thic fireplace
    An' commenced ta szwip once more.
'E screwed on four more rods an'
    Stuffed thic brush up further,
But from thic neighbour stuck out back
    'Eard wus not a murmer.
Meanwhile a mon from off the 'ill
    Was riding inta town,
When suddenly a sight 'im saw
    Which caused thic mon ta frown.
As 'im were going down 'ill
    'Im met a brush 'alfway,
Connected ta a length o' rod
    'Bout 'alf a mile away.

'Im traced the rod ta cottage
　　The soot 'e now could smell,
An' found thic brush a stickin' out
　　From where thic brick 'ad vell.
"Is 'im through", old 'Arry yelled
　　Ta the neighbour out the back,
"There's still no sign", 'er 'ollered back
　　"Thee's sure thee's got the knack?".
Thic mon 'e climbed from off 'is bike
　　An' knocked on cottage door,
An' said ta 'Arry "Be that thy brush
　　There — 'alfway up the 'ill?"
"Zurry", said 'Arry in disbelief
　　An' wiped 'is brow wi' soot,
"I thought thic stack were in the air
　　About a oighty foot".
Five 'ole 'ours 'e 'ad been there
　　A shovin' poles up 'igh,
If 'im 'ad shoved up many more
　　'Im would 'ave szwep the sky.
Old 'Arry pulled thic brush down
　　'Im were in a proper state,
'E'd started work at ten ta four
　　An' now 'twere 'alf past eight.
The neighbour came ta thank 'im
　　Fer szwippin' out 'er flue,
'Er give 'im two an' sixpence an'
　　'Im told 'er what ta do.
'Im picked 'is bag o' soot up
　　An' stormed off through the door,
An' swore ta them assembled that
　　'E would be a szwip no more.

COLOURS

GLORIOUS mosaic of old autumn browns
Unspoilt by the dust of the work-a-day towns,
Perfection beyond any old master's dreams
Beautiful portrait, oh rich forest scenes.
Profusions of grandeur in reds golds and browns
Nature's young trees clothed in nature's fine
                                        gowns.
Enriched by the sunlight that streams through
                                    the leaves
The glades they lie dying and yet no man grieves.
For the glory of death shall be followed in spring,
By the young greens of birth and the new life
                                    they bring.
The cycle of colour to live and to die,
May we drink in thy beauty before we pass by.

THERE BYUNT NOTHIN' LIKE GOOD ALE!

There byunt nothin' like good ale.
There byunt nothin' like good ale.
Thee c'ost kip thee tea an' coffee 'cause
There byunt nothin' like good ale.
Thee c'ost sup thee pint an' blind a bit
An' argue all night along,
Thee c'ost laugh an' shout an' stamp thee vit
An' thee c'ost sing a song.
But when thee's be through wi' all o' that
An' quietly wi' yer pint be sat,
Thee's gotta nod thee yud an' say that:
There byunt nothin' like good ale.
There byunt nothin' like good ale.

COAL MINING
A tribute to the Forest of Dean Miner

BLACK harvest gleaned from the belly of earth,
For thee we seek.
That sweat we offer — a mark of thy worth,
Yet we are weak.
Rude hands that claw at your dark rugged walls,
Dim eyes that peer through the dust of your falls,
That craving for comfort how strongly it calls,
Of thee we speak.

Gone are the days of our fathers before,
For thee they sought.
Small though their yields yet sufficient the more
Thy face they wrought.
Simple their methods and basic their need,
Unspoilt by demand of others' base greed,
From the fruit of their knowledge they
                              planted the seed,
From which we're taught.

31

But with the coming of machine and its power,
An age had gone.
What they won by week was now gathered by hour,
But their light shone.
But when that new era was profit no more,
And all that were left were the tiny and poor,
With nought but the skills of those days of yore,
You still go on.

VAREST SHIP

Wooly yudded varest ship
    Thee's got more rights than I,
Thee co'st wander where thee's please
    Where I must pass on by.

Thee can't be 'alf as stupid
    As you da vust appear,
'Cause no one ever bothers thee
    Or so it do appear.

If thee da lie down in the road
    An' 'ave theeself a kip,
No one ever moves thee on
    'Cause thee bist varest ship.

Thee do'snt work ta get thee bread
    Thee do'snt rise at seven,
If I was free as thee be free
    I'd think I was in 'eaven.

Wooly yudded varest ship
    I wish I was one too,
Then I could wander through the woods,
    Side by side with you.

MORNING

THE tired eyes of hasty night;
Short — sweet — sleep.
Peering into hazy morn that
Wakened to the song of birds — bite of frost —
                                    dew of night,
The world at peace with time.
But for an hour. For soon smoke must rise,
Transport move — commerce start the wheels
Of ardent day rolling ever rolling till,
The peace of morn lies trodden 'neath the
                                    brutal heel of day.
But for now; for one sweet hour
The tired eyes alone can share
The crystal pureness of their morn.

EVENING

THE trader's door is closed,
  The shadows lengthen.
The lofty hands at seven.
  The street is empty,
'Tis early yet for merriment;
  The home still keeps.
The fervent day is resting.
  Short sweet rest
Beneath the amber sky that
  Sooths day into night.

NATURE'S HARVEST

When my eyes no longer see
The hills and vales so dear to me,
And ears no longer hear birds sing
And gone the perfumes breathed in spring.
When legs grow tired of wooded lanes
And cease to run from summer rains,
And lips no longer talk with pride
Of this my lovely countryside.

Then let me lie deep in that earth
That to all beauty loved gave birth,
Where eyes no longer shall grow dim
And tiredness rule each weary limb.
How gently nature treats her own
When gathering in each seed she's sown,
To hold her children now at rest
So safely to her mother breast.

Albert's Dree Wi'ker

ALBERT'S DREE WI'KER

Old Albert loved 'is garden, it were 'is pride an' joy,
'Im 'ad loved it vram the time w'en 'e were just a little bwoy,
An every Easter Vriday off ta 'is shed 'e'd go,
Ta git 'is vark an' shovel, 'is dibbler an' 'is 'oe.

'Im 'ad got a good 'alf oicre, 'twere a tidy bit,
An' diggin' an' a 'oein' did kip old Albert vit.
'Im troubled not if it were wet or even freezin' cawld,
For tho' 'e now wer' zeventy dree; 'im wer' like a two year old.

'Im loved ta dig 'is garden, 'im loved ta pull up weeds,
'Im loved ta spread manure, 'im loved ta plant 'is zeeds.
'Im loved ta 'oe potatus; of this 'e'd never tire,
But best of all 'e really loved a stinkin' gert couch vire.

'E zet ta work a roikin' an' gatherin' rubbish up,
An' wen 'e'd finished roikin' 'im 'ad got a tidy yup.
Couch-grass, docks an' nettles, cabbage stumps an' all,
In a gert big yup 'im roiked 'em, up agyun the wall.

'Im stood back ta admire it an' 'ave 'iself a fag,
Then strolled up ta the garden shed ta vetch an oily rag.
Then returnin' ta 'is garden yup 'e placed thic rag inside,
Then struck a match an' lit the rag an' zome grass as 'e 'ad dried.

Thic 'eap began a smokin', just a bit at vust,
Then zuddenly thic yup broke up an' out a black cloud bust.
A black cloud vull o' zoot an' a stinkin' awful zmell,
That brought a zmile ta Albert's vace: ver 'im were gwain well.

41

Very zoon the street were black 's though night 'ad come
    bit zoon,
Puzzled neighbours looked aloft ta try ta zee the moon,
Sheets an' blankuts washed thic doy an' 'ung ta dry out back,
Sparklin' white thar billowin', zuddenly turned black.

The neighbours shut thar windus ta try ta kip it back,
But the filthy stinkin' odour wen' droo the smallest crack.
Old people choked an' spluttered an' little babies cried,
The swallus wen' back wum agyun; an' dogs ran off ta 'ide.

Doy a'ter doy Alb piled it on ta kip the blighter gwain,
Then wi' a wry contended zmile 'ould goo back ta 'is 'oein'.
Unaware that all around wus panic, grief an' sufferin',
As Albert's pile o' stinkin' muck slowly wen' on smoulderin'.

By the third wi'k 'im 'ad quietened an' the zmoke wuz not
    sa thick,
An' the ouses weren't sa dirty; an' the neighbours not sa zick.
An' Albert's ground wus planted wi' 'is zeeds up droo
    the ground,
As 'e loi back in 'is deckchoir, peace at last 'e'd vound.

'Im loi thar in 'is deckchoir reflectin' on 'i's pile,
An' reckoned ta 'iself as thic were best'n by a mile.
A dree wi'ker 'im 'ad managed ver the vust time in 'is life,
Despite loosin all 'i's neighbours 'i's whipput an' 'i's wife.

'ANDEL'S MEZZIAH

We allus went to chapel when we wuz little bwoys,
The one day 'o the wick when we'd putt awoy our toys,
Putt on our Zundy clobber wi polished bwoots an' all,
An' zet off ver the chapel veelin' ten vutt tall.

Ou Mother ployed the argan on Zundys, twice a doy.
'Er wuz nifty on the keyboard, 'Er could really ploy.
'Im were the type o' argan that's allus pumped by 'and,
'Far Mother could ztrike up wi' "Thar is a 'appy land".

A pumpin' o' thic argan wuz allus our job,
An' ver our Zundy effort we'd get a couple a bob.
Dree Imms an' a vesper an' a anthem vrom the choir,
Not enough ta raise a sweat, of this we'd never tire.

Never that wuz till Autumn; when things got rather wus,
The choir 'ould assemble an' all start ta rehearse.
Thoy did 'Andels Messiah wi' out foil every year,
A nightmare ver us pumpers; 'twere mar than we could bear.

Dree long 'ours a pumpin' wuz our lot fer zeven wick,
Dree long 'ours of 'ell that brought the colour ta yer cheeks,
An' blisters on yer 'ands an' cramp in muscles that yer'd vound,
As the choir bellowed loudly: "Let the trumpet zound".

Zo p'raps that wuz the reason why it took many years,
Ta appreciate good music an' abolish fears
Of 'Andels Mezziah an' all them sufferin' doys,
Endured every Autumn by us argan pumpin' bwoys.

VAREST NATIONAL ANTHEM

Thou ousnt vind a warmer welcome if thou's travel ver an' wide,
Thou cousnt 'ave a better comrade than a butty by yer zide,
Fer the Varest's 'eaven on earth,
Every mon da know it's wuth,
Zinging 'ow bizt thee awld butty; an' 'ow bist gwain on?
'Ow bist gwain on?
'Ow bist gwain on?
Zinging 'ow bist thee awld butty; an' 'ow bist gwain on?

IVOR AND THE ELEPHANT

On 'is woy ta work wuz Ivor,
'Alf past vive – the early shift.
All around wuz gloom an' darkness
As Ivor pedalled droo the mist.

On 'im went droo Devils Chapel,
Yudlights 'ardly cuttin' droo,
Wi' 'is yud down; pedallin' madly,
Speedin' down the road 'im new.

Round a corner raced our Ivor,
Hardly slowin' up at all.
Till 'im landed in the roadwoy,
An' thought that 'im 'ad 'it a wall.

Got up vram the grit an' gravel,
Picked 'is bike up vram the vloor.
Shone 'is light back up the roadwoy
Could not believe the zight 'im zaw.

Lumberin' slowly up the roadwoy
An elephant wuz on a stroll.
On 'iz woy ta Bream 'im yudded,
Up the 'ill t'wards Maypole.

Ivor zhook 'is yud in 'mazement,
Climbed back on 'is bike in doubt.
Zet off agyun on down t'wards Lydney,
Wondering if 'is wits wuz out.

Then in met a mon vram zircus
'Oo ztopped Ivor in 'is track.
Exed'n if 'im d'zin the wer'bouts
Of an elephant way back.

"Oi", zed Ivor in annoyance
As 'e give thic mon a frown.
"Thee'z wun a toik mar care o' Jumbo,
I nearly knocked thic blighter down".

* WARREN JAMES: FREEDOM FIGHTER

Warren James wer' sart o' mon
As allus zin as right wus done.
All 'is life 'im'd zin vair ploy,
An' feared not any mon nar bwoy.
But Warren 'im wer' up in arms,
An' zet off round the 'oods an' varms.
Gatherin' all 'is mates around,
'Im tawld 'em all what 'im 'ad vound.
"All the land be venced", 'im zed,
"Wer once our ship an' pigs wus ved.
Time a come ta make a stand,
An' toik the vences from the land.
All our rights 'll disappear
Lest we da stop it now; right 'ere".
All agreed ta meet thic night,
When thoy ud start ta putt things right.
Stroke o' twelve thoy all met up,
Ten er twelve; a tidy yup.
Off thoy went inta the night,
Each one wus spoilin' fer a vight.
Zoon thoy come ta trouble spot.
An' zet about ta shift the lot.
Very zoon thar work was done,
An' off thoy zet once more fer wum.
All the common land thoy'd vreed,
Once mar thar pigs an' ship could veed.
In the marnin' sharp at oight,
A mon cum droow old Warrens goit.
Rattled 'ard upon 'is door,
An' zhook the 'ouse vrum ruf ta vloor.
Warren opened up ta zee
What all the noise outback could be.

50

Then 'im zin the local sqire,
Oo'd come ta give our vreind the wire.
Less 'is tricks 'e did curtoil,
Then 'im 'ould vind 'izself in joil.
Warren gathered up 'is men,
An' tawld 'em plainly thar an' then
What could 'appen ta 'em all
If thoy ztill wen' agyun the law.
To a mon thoy did agree,
The zorry business droo thoy'd zee.
'Elp wuz needed right awoy,
If thoy were gwain ta win the doy.
Mar an' mar thoy gathered in,
Till thoy 'ad got enough ta win.
Off then zet the merry band,
Ta drag mar vences frum the land.
But thee's time; ta thar dismoy,
A bunch a so'jers blocked thar woy.
Mon took off wi'out a vight,
An' Warren James 'im tuk ta vlight.
Wen thoy went ta serve the writ,
Thoy vount'n 'idin' in a pit.
Took 'n var a cart a law,
An' zentenced 'im before 'em all,
Zo the zentence ver 'is crime,
Wus transportation ver all time.
All 'is matez was zad an' grave,
But vrom thic time no trouble gave.
In the end thoy changed the law,
An' Warren got a pardon call.
But Warren James n'er came wum,

An' never zid 'is mates agyun.
But remembered ta thee's doy,
The "Freedom" mon as zhowed the woy

*Warren James was transported to
Tasmania as punishment for the part
he played in the riots of 1831.*

BILLY THE BANDSMON

Billy wer' a shart ass,
Jus' vive vut off the ground,
An' Billy was a bandsmon,
The best 'brass drum' around.

'Zilver Brass'wuz marching',
At this thoy wuz the best,
Wi' Billy right be'ind 'em,
'Is bass drum on 'is chest.

Thic drum wer' big as Billy,
An' strapped upon 'is chest,
Poor Billy 'ad no inklin',
Of the wer'bouts of the rest.

Stroit roads wuz no problem,
'Im jus' kep' gwain oin,
But crosswords wus a yudache
Fer this poor drummer mon.

Zoon thoy reached a junction,
Decision time 'ad come,
Lef' wen' 'Zilver Prize', an' right
Wen' Billy an' 'is drum.

'Zilver Prize' wuz flummoxed,
Thar leader called "Vall Out",
Thoy looked up back ver drummer,
But Billy wuz not about.

Billy kep' on gwain,
Thumpin' fer all 'is might,
Lef' right, lef' right marchin' on
Off inta the night.

Off o'er 'ill an' valley,
O'er moor and mountain crest,
Wonderin' when the shout 'ould come,
Ta stop an' 'ave a rest.

Thoy never vound poor Billy,
Though rumours flew quite thick,
Zomeone 'ad zeen 'im drummin',
Ten mile narth o' Wick.

If thouse zee a bandsmon,
A marchin' wi' a drum,
Turn 'n round an' point'n back
The woy back to 'is wum.

GUZZLIN' STUNNEM

Jarge wuz fond o' 'stunnem'
A filthy evil brew,
An' didn't care a tinkers cuss
'Bout the damage it 'ould do.

'Im guzzled it in 'im reg'lar,
T'were is one delight,
Ten pints every marnin'
An' another ten at night.

It made'n feel quite 'appy
As quietly 'im did zit,
Losin' all inhibitions
An' the use of both 'is vit.

'Is body velt quite peaceful,
But from the waist down 'im were djud,
No sense o' veelin' in 'is legs
An' not much in 'is yud.

Jarge 'ad 'ad a zkinvull,
'Is guzzlin' it were done,
An' thar an' then decided
'Im 'ad better yud fer wum.

'Im putt 'is empty mug down
An' looked towards the door,
An' got up vram thic table
An' collapsed upon the vloor.

'Is mates thoy went ta 'elp'n
An' got'n to 'is vit,
An enquired of 'im wi' zome concern,
"Jarge, c'ost walk a bit?"

'Im took a shart step voward
An dree gert big 'uns back,
Then spun around an' 'it the wall
An' give both shins a crack.

Thoy took'n ta the doorwoy
An' faced'n up the 'ill,
An' told'n ta goo steady
Or 'im ood 'ave a spill.

'Im thanked 'em all ver 'elpin'
An' waved 'em all good-doy,
Then staggered out inta the road
An' zet off t'other woy.

'Is pace it did get vaster
As 'e lurched between the trees,
Leanin' at an angle
'Bout a varty vive degrees.

'Im 'it a gert big oak tree
Wi' a loud resoundin' smack,
An' spun around an' shook is yud
Then started 'is woy back.

'E began ta veel quite drowsy
The result of all 'is booze,
An' thought 'e'd get 'is yud down
An' 'ave 'iself a snooze.

'E lay down in the roadwoy
In the kerb 'e putt 'is feet,
Wi' a catseye ver a pilla
An' 'is jackut ver a sheet.

Meanwhile a buz was comin'
Takin' the nightshift 'ome ta bed,
An' vast thoy was approachin'
Wer ol' Jarge wus peacefully laid.

When thoy zin 'im in thar yudlights
Thoy stopped thic buz real quick,
An' wen across ta Jarge ta zee
If 'im wer djud or zick.

Jarge wuz snarlin' like a good'n
Wi' a wry contented zmile,
'Twere as well as 'e wus 'appy
'Cos 'e'd be thar a while.

The blokes strolled round about'n
Thoy'd 'ad a proper vright,
But wen thoy sniffed the evenin' air
Thoy understood old Jarge's plight.

Wen them blokes 'ad all decided
That dear old Jarge 'adn't died,
Thoy lifted'n up between 'em
An' putt 'im in the zide.

Thoy climed back on thar buz
An' drove off 'ome ta bed,
An' left old Jarge a snoozin'
On 'is tarmacadam bed.

Wen Jarge woke up next marnin'
The zun wuz shinin' bright,
'is shirt an' zocks was wringin' wet
Frum the dew that vell that night.

'E got up vram thic kerbzide
An' stretched an' 'ad a think,
An' pondered which 'e needed most
'Is breakfast or a drink.

'E looked up t'wards 'is cottage
An' down t'wards pub door,
Then takin' a virm decision
Jarge strolled down ta 'ave zome more.

* ELI HATTON'S CURSE

Thoy 'ung Eli Hatton on Pingry Tump
Thoy 'ung 'im ver murder thoy zoy,
An' the curse that Eli bestowed on thic town
Remains thar ta thee's very doy.

Toy 'ung 'im in zummertime zo thoy da zoy
Unrepentant an' vull o' 'ate,
Gibbeted 'e wus on the top of a 'ill
A savage an' terrible fate.

The zunlight shone bright as thoy strung Eli up
An' vlooded the 'illtop wi' light,
An' ver miles around everybody cud zee
Old Eli an' 'is zorry plight.

A'far meetin' 'is maker 'im lifted 'is yud
An' shouted thee's curse loud an' clear,
"A curse on you people; your markut an' town
I swear ver thee's deed thou'll poy dear".

Wi' that 'im grew quiet an' passed on 'is woy
'Is shoutin' an cursin' were done,
'Im 'ung thar quite peaceful the rest o' the doy
At rest in the warm zummer zun.

'Im 'ung thar vour doys in that warm zummer zun
Round 'is vit the kiddies did ploy,
Till the temperature got a bit out o' 'and
An' Eli did start ta decoy.

In the town down below the markut wus vull
O' varmers a sellin' thar wares,
Prime biff, park an' mutton ver which thoy wus famed
Ducks, rabbuts an' cockrels an' 'ares.

The people 'ould travel vram miles around
Ta purchase this prime 'ome-grown meat,
Zum vivty or zixty 'ad walked inta town
Ignorin' the strength zappin' 'eat.

Meanwhile on thic 'illzide old Eli 'ad guests
Attracted; no doubt; by the zmell,
'Bout zix million 'ouse vlies was buzzin' around
An' varty blue-bottles as well.

Thoy zoon zin off Eli an' then vlew around
Ta plan out the rest o' thar doy,
'Twas then that thoy noticed thic markut below
An' decided that's wer' thoy'd stoy.

Thoy vlew off tagether an' zet off down 'ill
An' vell fram the sky like a cloud,
Thoy buzzed round thic markut fram one end ta t'other
'For zettlin' down on the crowd.

In no time at all thic markut wus bare
No butchers, no people, no meat,
No tradin', no profit, no business, no 'ope
Jus' blue-bottles, 'ouse vlies an' 'eat.

Folks never wen' back ta thic markut agyun
Business got progressively worse,
An' townsfolk 'ould glance at the top o' thic 'ill
An' damn Eli Hatton's vowed curse.

Thoy 'ung Eli Hatton on Pingry Tump
Thoy 'ung 'im ver murder thoy soy,
An' the curse that Eli bestowed on thic town
Remains thar ta thee's very doy.

*Many years ago, Eli Hatton was hung on a hill
overlooking the village of Mitcheldean. It is said that
the decline of the market in the village was due to
the flies that were attracted to Eli's corpse as it
decayed, and subsequently infecting the meat on
sale in the market.*

THE GREY LADY

Thar's many a story tawld,
An' 'ghost' yarns be best I da zoy,
But the scariest tale of 'em all,
Is of Ralph an' the Lady in Grey.

'Is tastes wus zimple an' vew,
An' ta zeek both freedom an' vun,
'E'd 'ave a vour mile stroll ta the pub,
An' a vour mile stroll back agyun.

The strollin' was good fer 'is 'ealth,
But not zo the time spent between,
An' wen time come fer Ralph ta depart,
The back o' ten pints 'im 'ad zeen.

Outzide the weather wuz cawld,
The wind blowin' up to a gale,
As 'ome on 'iz vour mile stroll,
Wen' Ralph an' 'iz ten pints o' ale.

Off droo the village 'im strolled,
Past the churchyard now zodden wi' roin,
An' the zound o' the wind in 'is years,
Ployed tricks on Ralph's fuddled broin.

Fram thic churchyard a voice 'e cud 'ear,
A loud ghostly voice as did scare,
Barn on the wind an' the starm,
"Tread Lightly" the voice did declare.

'Tread lightly' wuz least on Ralph's mind,
As 'ot vut ver wum 'e did run.
Up droo the vields an' the kilns
Wer' the night shift 'ad shartly begun.

Willum worked 'ard droo the night,
W'en most be tucked inta thar bed,
Slavin' awoy at them kilns,
Stoppin' but once ver 'is bread.

'Is mother; a lovely ol' zole,
Thought the world o' Willum 'er zon,
An' each night 'er took'n 'is bread,
Jus' as zoon an 'er bakin' wer' done.

'Twus approachin' a quater ta twelve,
W'en is mother delivered Will's bread,
In the vog an' the gloom o' the night,
Wi' the roin lashin' wet round 'er yud.

'Er bade 'er Willum "Goodnight",
An' gathered 'er grey skirts round tight,
An' wi' 'er grey shaw round 'er yd,
Zet off agyun inta the night.

Ralph 'ad stopped runnin' by now,
The 'ill 'ad zapped all o' 'is breath.
Pantin' 'e leant on a vence,
Ta prolong the onset o' death.

As 'e gazed inta the night,
A zight met 'iz bleary eyed stare,
In the midst o' the vog an' the gloom,
A ghostly grey lady wus there.

Poor Ralph 'e cum out in a zweat,
An' both knees trembled wi' fear,
As the ghostly figure in grey,
Came nearer and nearer and near.

By now panic 'ad taken a grip,
An' the name o' the game wus survival,
'E raced t'wards wum wi' a shriek,
Wer' 'is missus 'ould greet 'is arrival.

'E crashed droo the door in a rush,
An' collapsed in a yup in a chair,
'Iz missus exed wer' 'im 'ad bin,
But by now Ralph couldn't care.

'E started ta tell 'er the truth,
'Bout the voice an' the lady in grey,
But 'is missus 'er wasn't impressed,
An' clobbered poor Ralph wi' a tray.

Ralph often went boozin' agyun,
But wi'out all previous vuss,
Fer 'e never did walk wum agyun,
'E allus caught the last buz.

ZUPPER AT THE LOCAL

A big red spotted 'anky,
'Alf a loaf o' bread,
A lump o' Double Glawster,
Onion big's yer 'ead,
A qwart o' two o' zider,
Zupper ver a mon,
Zat wi' all yer butties,
W'en all yer work be done.

SONG OF THE WYE VALLEY

There is a picture in my heart,
It's blazened deep within,
More perfect than the painters art,
It's beauty cannot dim.

There is no bauble, land or crown,
Whose value can compare,
There is no price that man can place
Upon this jewel we share.

To those who search the scriptures texts,
To learn of Eden's place,
Come see! it's here in majesty,
In beauty, life and grace.

NIGHT

The black curtain of day is drawn
Slowly across the windows of our toil,
Man rests, reflects, communicates with his maker,
Sinks into blessed oblivion.
Problems for a moment forgotten
Along with the troubles of the world.
The mind rests,
The soul does not.
The Lord looks down, smiles benignly on his sleeping child,
Separated for a moment from the evils of the world,
Till the curtains are drawn once again
Letting in the light and ills of dawn.

I DIDN'T REALISE (IN BOYHOOD DAYS)

I didn't realise in boyhood days that things were not that way,
The world was not the place that the schoolbooks seemed to say,
With justice, peace and freedom for some an unknown thing,
And people not one nation with one eternal King.

I didn't realise in boyhood days; Earths not for me and you,
The woods and fields and rivers were owned by just a few,
That man was just a slave from the day he first breathed air,
Years of toil and years of strife for just a meagre share.

I didn't realise in boyhood days that race was not a game,
That pretty coloured children weren't children just the same
That grew up to be men just as any child would do,
But scorned by those around them; those of a different hue.

I didn't realise in boyhood days 'the world' meant disarray,
With subversion, fear and tyranny for some; a normal day,
With nothing for the future 'cept a trust in their dear Lord,
Through him their own salvation, their peace and their accord.

PROPOSITION

A man; asleep; lay dreaming,
It was a vivid dream,
He dreamt he was a butterfly,
The prettiest moth you'd seen.

He flew around in sunshine,
An idyllic life was this,
A world of light and beauty,
Of contentment, peace and bliss.

On waking from his slumber,
He thought of what he'd dreamt,
So vivid was the memory,
He pondered what it meant.

Was he a man who, dreaming,
A butterfly became,
Or a butterfly who, dreaming,
Became a man – the same?

HE HAD NO WAY OF TELLING!

HOMECOMINGS

The bands played "Rule Brittania",
The bunting swirled around,
The crowds cheered from the dockside,
The boys were homeward bound.

Returning conquering heroes,
The mighty ship drew near,
Falling from each welcoming eye,
A shameless salt-proud tear.

A short speech from the Admiral,
A handshake from the Queen,
A medal for a corporal,
A hero of Goose Green.

A welcome fit for heroes,
No less than they deserved,
A credit to their calling,
And the nation they had served.

The weeks and months passed swiftly,
Once more the ship neared shore,
Again the people waited,
Far fewer than before.

There was no "Rule Brittania",
No bunting over head,
No handshake from Her Majesty,
No words of welcome said.

You can't hear "Rule Brittania",
You can't see flags o'er head,
You can't grasp a welcoming handshake,
When your in a pine box, DEAD.

TO LEONARD CLARK

You are no longer with us,
Our Loss,
His gain,
We are richer for your days with us
Full and many.
They are no more.
Yet you will always be with us,
You cannot leave,
You cannot be forgotten,
So much of you remains.
Your heart is in our keeping,
Accessible to all who new and all who seek to know
The one who understood.